CW00342636

THE
SAGITTARIUS
ORACLE

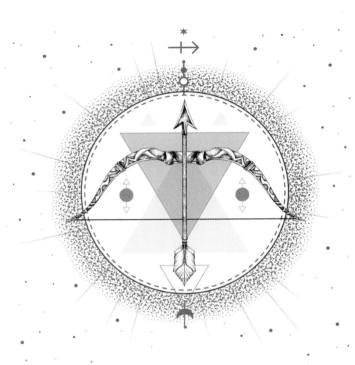

THE
SAGITTARIUS
ORACLE

INSTANT ANSWERS FROM
YOUR COSMIC SELF

STELLA FONTAINE

greenfinch

Introduction

Welcome to your zodiac oracle, carefully crafted especially for you Sagittarius, and brimming with the wisdom of the universe.

Is there a tricky-to-answer question niggling at you and you need an answer?

Whenever you're unsure whether to say 'yes' or 'no', whether to go back or to carry on, whether to trust or to turn away, make some time for a personal session with your very own oracle. Drawing on your astrological profile, your zodiac oracle will guide you in understanding, interpreting and answering those burning questions that life throws your way. Discovering your true path will become an enlightening journey of self-actualization.

Humans have long cast their eyes heavenwards to seek answers from the universe. For millennia the sun, moon and stars have been our constant companions as they repeat their paths and patterns across the skies. We continue to turn to the cosmos for guidance, trusting in the deep and abiding wisdom of the universe as we strive for fulfilment, truth and understanding.

The most basic and familiar aspect of astrology draws on the twelve signs of the zodiac, each connected to a unique constellation as well as its own particular colours, numbers and characteristics. These twelve familiar signs are also known as the sun signs: Aries, Taurus, Gemini, Cancer, Leo, Virgo, Libra, Scorpio, Sagittarius, Capricorn, Aquarius and Pisces.

Aries   Taurus   Gemini   Cancer   Leo   Virgo

Libra   Scorpio   Sagittarius   Capricorn   Aquarius   Pisces

Each sign is associated with an element (fire, air, earth or water), and also carries a particular quality: cardinal (action-takers), fixed (steady and constant) and mutable (changeable and transformational). Beginning to understand these complex combinations, and to recognize the layered influences they bring to bear on your life, will unlock your own potential for personal insight, self-awareness and discovery.

In our data-flooded lives, now more than ever it can be difficult to know where to turn for guidance and advice. With your astrology oracle always by your side, navigating life's twists and turns will become a smoother, more mindful process. Harness the prescience of the stars and tune in to the resonance of your sun sign with this wisdom-packed guide that will lead you to greater self-knowledge and deeper confidence in the decisions you are making. Of course, not all questions are created equal; your unique character, your circumstances and the issues with which you find yourself confronted all add up to a conundrum unlike any other... but with your question in mind and your zodiac oracle in your hand, you're already halfway to the answer.

Sagittarius
NOVEMBER 22 TO DECEMBER 21

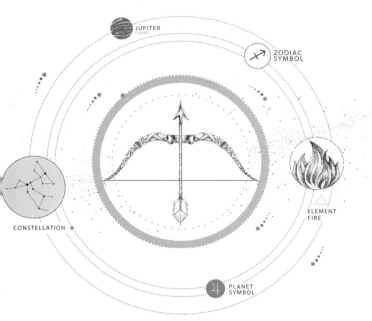

JUPITER
PLANET

ZODIAC
SYMBOL

ELEMENT
FIRE

CONSTELLATION

PLANET
SYMBOL

Element: Fire

Quality: Mutable

Named for the constellation: Sagittarius (the archer)

Ruled by: Jupiter

Opposite: Gemini

Characterized by: Idealism, humour, freedom

Colour: Blue

How to Use This Book

You can engage with your oracle whenever you
need to but, for best results, create an atmosphere
of calm and quiet, somewhere you will not be
disturbed, making a place for yourself and your
question to take priority. Whether this is a particular
physical area you turn to in times of contemplation,
or whether you need to fence off a dedicated space
within yourself during your busy day, that all
depends on you and your circumstances. Whichever
you choose, it is essential that you actively put other
thoughts and distractions to one side in order to
concentrate upon the question you wish to answer.

Find a comfortable position, cradle this book lightly
in your hands, close your eyes, centre yourself. Focus
on the question you wish to ask. Set your intention
gently and mindfully towards your desire to answer
this question, to the exclusion of all other thoughts
and mind-chatter. Allow all else to float softly away,
as you remain quiet and still, gently watching the
shape and form of the question you wish to address.
Gently deepen and slow your breathing.

Tune in to the ancient resonance of your star sign, the vibrations of your surroundings, the beat of your heart and the flow of life and the universe moving in and around you. You are one with the universe.

Now simply press the book between your palms as you clearly and distinctly ask your question (whether aloud or in your head), then open it at any page. Open your eyes. Your advice will be revealed.

Read it carefully. Take your time turning this wisdom over in your mind, allowing your thoughts to surround it, to absorb it, flow with it, then to linger and settle where they will.

Remember, your oracle will not provide anything as blunt and brutal as a completely literal answer. That is not its role. Rather, you will be gently guided towards the truth you seek through your own consciousness, experience and understanding. And as a result, you will grow, learn and flourish.

Let's begin.

Close your eyes.

Hold the question you want
answered clearly in your mind.

Open your oracle to any page to
reveal your cosmic insight.

As one of the most nature-loving signs, remember to take some time outside. Breathe it in Sagittarius, and reset yourself.

Although it doesn't quite fit with your spontaneous approach to life, this time you should acknowledge that there is likely only one acceptable outcome. Don't worry, it doesn't mean you suddenly need to settle and become stagnant... but do proceed with caution.

When you know what it is you really want, there is nothing more powerful than that dead-straight aim Sagittarius is so famous for.

Your fabulous Sagittarius swagger means you are often certain you know best. And, let's be honest, you're usually right! But bring some patience and empathy to this situation; take a little more time over it and check your perspective.

Born to explore, you need freedom and possibility built into all you do Sagittarius. Boundaries don't really work for you. Others will need to find a way to get their heads around that.

Potential travel companions are never in short supply; who wouldn't want to join exciting adventures laced with possibility? But finding the right one, well, that might prove more difficult. Make space for intuition and allow it to guide you.

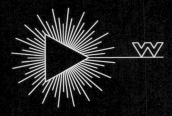

Neither patience nor
perseverance come easily to you,
but both are extremely useful skills to
harness. They could be the key to your
success this time.

Embrace risk rather than
fleeing it Sagittarius; reward awaits
on the other side.

Hold your heart and your mind
open to the possibilities that lie ahead.
Change is on your horizon, but there is
nothing you can yet do to plan for it.
Be ready.

Don't be tempted to hold
tightly to everything that comes
your way Sagittarius – plenty is meant
to just pass through on its way to
somewhere else.

If you feel bounded by bad
energy and negativity, move to
protect yourself with a little distance.
Do not allow others to restrict your
horizons or limit your options.

Charming, enthusiastic, energetic
and full of fun, you have everything
you need already to hand Sagittarius.
Step forwards into this adventure
with courage and conviction;
don't look back.

Breathe deeply and let it go.

Trust your instincts Sagittarius, they rarely let you down. Your first impulse was the right one – now is not the time for second-guessing yourself. Persevere.

Be generous with the knowledge
and resources you have gathered
recently Sagittarius; there are plenty
around you who could benefit.

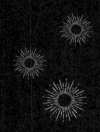

Sagittarian communication skills are strong and effective; put them to work and share what you know. You may be pleasantly surprised with what comes back to you.

The sensation of being out of control can cause you to feel stressed and perhaps even anxious. But there is a clean and absolute beauty in the moment you realize that you cannot change things; relinquishing the desire for control will free you.

If you have been turning this one
over in your mind for a while now, it
might be time to let it go or to place it
in the 'unsolvable for now' pile.
Time for a change.

Sags love a challenge almost
as much as you love an adventure.
But along the way, don't forget
that taking a relatively sensible
approach to the risks involved
does not equate to weakness.
Look out for yourself.

It is perhaps time to adjust your approach to this one... inconceivable though it is, there is a chance you might have been wrong at first. Decide to view this as a chance to learn and move forwards.

You will very likely need some help with this one. Luckily, you are surrounded by a solid fanbase, so employ it to good effect now. Just don't forget to say 'thank you' afterwards.

If you are disappointed about a particular situation, event or issue that has arisen, take some time to examine the base of this emotion and the attachment you have to it. Perhaps there is a deeper negativity you are struggling to process?

Release that which doesn't serve you.

Motivated and thrill-loving
are two archer traits that complement
each other particularly well. Putting in
the time and effort virtually
guarantees that you will reap the
kinds of rewards you value
most highly Sagittarius.

Prioritize your loved ones and nurture your relationships, rather than allowing your attention to be distracted by what looks like an easy strike. This one is not for you.

There is every likelihood that
this will not be the smoothest journey,
but really your passport is already
stamped and you're halfway to your
boarding gate. You might as well
persevere – one foot in front of the
other (and repeat), and you
will get there.

There's a lot going on here,
so many balls to juggle and plates
to spin, and of course there is no one
better at that than you. But you must
trust your stars; your path ahead is
already illuminated.

Time to step away from the things that stifle you, whether simply the tedium of a particular routine or that small-minded approach that certain people seem to circle back to.

Increasing opportunities will spring up all around you; even more so as you adopt a warm and encouraging attitude to others. While the leadership role holds little appeal for you Sagittarius, you have the perfect blend of skills to be the most brilliant role model.

You're a thrill-seeker Sagittarius, but your excitement-hunts can include what others might see as an unnerving level of uncertainty and risk. You definitely say 'yes' to the fun, but don't always want to be part of the planning committee.

The most important thing, when
faced with adversity, is the way you
choose to cope with it. With wonderful
Jupiter on your side, and the fire
within, there is nothing you cannot
turn to your favour if you
apply yourself.

There is a better way to go about this; it should not seem as difficult as it feels right now. A fresh approach is required Sagittarius. Don't lose heart, just pause, recalibrate and reset.

Throw that whip-sharp
Sagittarius intellect into high gear,
then sit back and enjoy the ride.
Possibility is more complex and
infinitely more beautiful than just
what you can see on the surface.

Your confident, clever approach
rarely fails you Sagittarius; don't be
tempted to do this anyone else's way,
for any reason. That said, the decision
to aim for a system-shaking change is
rarely made well on the toss of a
coin. Sleep on it.

Tackle this one head on and with
your compass properly set Sagittarius.
Once you have plotted your course
and begun, don't look back.

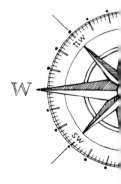

For the greatest chance
at contentment, channel that
incredible Sagittarius motivation
into commitment, connection
and closeness.

Keep your quiver well stocked and your arrows sharp Sagittarius. You never know when you might need them.

A focus on material things can weigh you down Sagittarius; they will not make you happy. A surfeit of possessions may instead have the opposite effect, increasing negativity and stress. Concentrate on what really matters, the irreplaceable things in your life.

Engaging, likeable, quick and clever
– you've got everything going for you
Sagittarius. Add to this your talents for
deep thinking and mental agility and
remember you almost always find a
happy solution. Trust yourself.

You are what you do, not what you say. Empty words and hollow promises don't sit well with you, whether you are on the giving or the receiving end. Don't be tempted to sidestep your own integrity – it has carried you this far and served you well.

Your fullest potential is not
to be found in a constant pursuit
of adventure, but in nurturing and
learning to understand those who
truly care about you. Which isn't to
say that you should forsake those
adventures... but maybe take
the others along for the ride
once in a while.

Those you love will be there with you as you face this next stage of challenges. Whether you see them or not, know that their energy is present.

Your Sagittarius skills for keen understanding, straightforward communication and quick adaptability will be in hot demand. Look ahead and focus on the future.

Another change will be along shortly, which should bring much excitement to your Sag heart. Remain alert and awake to new signs, and be sure you stay open to possibilities, rather than rushing ahead towards the promise of new scenery.

Your talent for getting straight
to the point is well-known Sagittarius;
forgo the fluff and the sugar-coating
and use this skill now.

Your instinct is strong.
Think less and act more.

Your quick thinking can sometimes lead you to hasty and unnecessarily harsh words. Remember to nurture those around you – doing a bit of essential maintenance on those bridges now and again will be much easier than rebuilding them when they start to crumble.

Don't forget to focus on your
breathing Sagittarius; for something
so basic and intrinsically important, it's
surprising how many people get it
completely wrong. Fill yourself up,
then a little bit more, then
let it all go. Repeat.

Confusing as this is to a
plain-speaker, your Sagittarian
gift for truth-telling sometimes goes
unappreciated. Lean into your intuition
this time and hold back. As well-meant
as they are, there is a chance your
words may be taken as
unwelcome criticism.

Give yourself a break. Even
though staying switched on and
firing on all cylinders can feel as vital
as breathing to a super-independent
Sagittarius, sometimes even you have
to dial it down for a bit.

Increased strategy would be a
good move for you Sagittarius;
especially given your usual impulse to
adopt a spontaneous approach to
pretty much everything you do. Others
may feel differently about it, but you
will have to leave their feelings with
them to untangle – it's not something
you can help them with.

It is unlikely anyone could ever accuse you of being boring. Or predictable, or, you know, cautious (the horror). But uncertain times call for quick and decisive action; now choose a direction and make a start.

Of course, anything is possible, especially for such a courageous, fired-up Sagittarius. But you might need to take a walk around this one, to observe it from new angles. The direction of approach will make the difference to your chances of success.

With your actions and emotions more often than not fastened together Sagittarius, it is important not to allow yourself to become weighed down or stuck. Keep it all moving and stay light and easy.

Circular thinking will not serve
you well Sagittarius. Do not spend
too much of your precious
time focusing on this.

With Jupiter in charge, the
biggest planet of all, it can be tough
trying to take a step back. But
sometimes you need to let all the buzz
carry on around you – a quick break
and you'll be back in the thick of
it in no time.

Your Sagittarian optimism will not necessarily help you win this time. It is important to consider what other people are thinking (perhaps without obsessing over the fact that they are clearly wrong), while at the same time accepting that you cannot control the feelings of others.

Let go of the effort and allow
things to be as they are. The knotty
ones usually have a way of eventually
working themselves smooth again.
And if they don't, they don't. That's
just the way of things.

If you are feeling restrained
or otherwise held back at the
moment Sagittarius, take some
time to check in with your emotions.
Try body-scanning to work out what
you are holding on to and how best
to work through and release it.

Allow your head to rule over
your heart on this occasion Sagittarius.
Make the decision clean, sharp
and logical.

Underneath the sparkling, outgoing exterior lies your complicated, paper-thin emotional layers, as delicate as an onion skin. To truly allow others to know you, you must allow them to understand this reality.

Now is not the right time to engage in complicated strategic process. Decide on a direction and just get moving.

You are a dynamic force,
clear-eyed and strong-armed, so
it can seem particularly disorienting
when events seem to be escaping
your grasp. Trust that there is a greater
plan at work right now. Breathe, stay in
the moment, relax your grip on that
you are seeking to hold and
this too shall pass.

Ruled by Jupiter, you love to be on the move, preferably at a pace, and hate to feel trapped or fixed. But be careful you're not zooming past this one too quickly. Look at it from another angle and you might find that you missed something pretty important first-time round.

Of course, you prefer the interesting questions, why would you waste your precious time on the boring bits? Life's too short, etc., etc. But are you sure this is really the question you want to answer?

Ask again.

Keep that adrenaline addiction in check Sagittarius; your own drive for bigger, higher, further, more may well need inspecting.

The expectations of others,
noisy and weighty as they can seem,
are not your concern Sagittarius. Hold
your line and dive in your own way –
ultimately, you are answerable
only to yourself.

You accumulate plenty of friends
and supporters, but sometimes you're
moving so quickly you don't notice
how many you are leaving behind in
your wake. Don't side-step your
impulse to maintain or rekindle
connections.

Keep one eye on the long-view Sagittarius, and remember you need to build a future as well as getting the most out of today.

Sagittarius is a super-charged fire sign and you need fuel in plentiful supply, as well as stacks of oxygen, to feed the flame. Get out into the fresh air today. Challenge yourself to a hard, uphill walk or a long run by the sea – the answer will reveal itself. This is a tricky one, but perhaps not for the reasons you think.

You know what you want
Sagittarius, and with the archer as
your constellation you're sure to hit
the mark. Just be sure you take careful
aim, to avoid collateral damage.

Quick, versatile and smart as you are, sometimes you need to take a pause and let the world catch up with you. There is something you still need to know; something you may miss if you keep racing on ahead.

Your natural inclination to prioritize thinking over feeling might not have served you well this time. It is important to investigate further. The details are not exactly as they might have seemed at first, fleeting glance – you will need to engage some empathy to understand the full picture.

Fuelling your flame with
negativity is short-sighted Sagittarius,
and a sure-fire way to burn out too
soon. Maintain your glow with a steady
supply of positive energy.

You Sagittarians are a lively bunch, full of fun and tremendously attractive company. But don't lose sight of your priorities in the middle of all the bustle. Commit yourself to what matters – build up your own understanding and resources, so you can become more self-reliant. Others won't always surround you.

Curiosity and imagination, wit and intelligence, your star sign has been very generous with your gifts Sagittarius. Time to employ them in pursuit of this goal.

Allowing others the time and
space to feel heard when they want
to engage with you can really test
your Sagittarian patience, especially if
it feels like they are insisting on your
attention for longer than you want to
give it. Really though, they are not
asking that much of you.

This is a tricky one and the details are not precisely as they seemed at first glance. Take a closer look – there may well be an inherent nuance that wasn't obvious to start with.

Truth and wisdom are always
right there with you Sagittarius, but
others are more likely to accept them
if you allow a little space and stillness
for them to settle. Gentle handling is
imperative if you are going to
sort this one out.

With Gemini as your opposite sign, sometimes you need to remember that a lighter touch can yield a cleaner outcome. Now is one of those times.

You don't need constant praise or feedback Sagittarius, and the fact you are so deeply self-motivated is what has brought you here in the first place. But if you are starting to feel uncertain, or even unanchored, especially in relation to your work, there is no harm in asking for some clarity or reassurance.

Your strongly positive, independent
streak means you are more than
willing to take a chance and more
likely than most to follow your heart
despite the opinions of others.
Stay true to yourself and
stand up for your beliefs.

You are strong on empathy, but
low on willingness to sugar-coat the
truth. This can spark some conflict, but
at the heart of the problem is a simple
fact: what others frame as 'tact', you
would describe as 'a lie'.

You are adventurous, courageous, up for any challenge and of course endlessly adaptable, but even you know that huge decisions about big changes are best not made on the spur of the moment. Sleep on this one Sagittarius.

You have little patience for emotional blackmail, and even less time for those who are wishy-washy and uncertain about their own opinions. Others trust you to tell them what you really think, even if they have to take a deep breath and steel themselves before asking. Remember though, you can perhaps deliver it a little more gently without watering it down.

You are always truthful, as well as generous and trustworthy. Imagination and a philosophical approach come naturally to you, and optimism and positivity guide almost everything you do. With all of this in your assets-bundle, no obstacle is insurmountable.

Tenacious as you are
Sagittarius, sometimes it can be
tempting to skim-read the problem.
Right now, a more comprehensive
understanding will ultimately simplify
your approach. Resist the urge to
distract yourself from the
task at hand.

With a reputation for trailblazing and fearlessness, now is the time to make the most of those Sagittarian talents. Do not shy away from this challenge. Nothing worth doing seems easy at first.

When it comes to roads diverging
in a wood, you always choose the least
travelled. Smart and capable, you love
nothing better than forging your own
path ahead. Remember to keep your
patience with those less bold than you
– they bring different wisdom and
you will benefit from it.

Pause to consider the lessons you are learning in all of this Sagittarius – your future approach will benefit from current experiences. Learn from the past and move swiftly onwards.

Your first impulse was the right one, although initially it may have seemed to make little sense. Step away from the over-thinking and go with it.

Spend some time focusing on yourself rather than your social circle right now Sagittarius. Pour your energies into creative outlets and hobbies; you may even discover a talent you didn't know you had.

It can be difficult for you to pause and take rest Sagittarius, but you need to handle this one calmly and with focus, especially if you want to deal with it properly. Seek advice and solace if you need it. Friends will be more than happy to listen.

Honesty and truth are key for you but, despite this, now and again a messy confusion does seem to make its way to your door. Resist the temptation to over-talk this one, just carry on with other things for the moment and check back in later to see whether it has sorted itself out.

If this path looks too challenging, consider whether what is likely at the end is really worth it. It is not too late to alter your course, to find a new road. Perhaps it is time for a shiny new adventure Sagittarius –
now isn't that tempting?

You already have all the knowledge
you need to make this decision.

Protecting your interests should
not be at the cost of your happiness
Sagittarius. Follow your heart and the
rest will fall into place.

You are an active listener, curious about others and intuitive enough to understand even the unsaid things. Others feel heard when they engage with you. But it is not always essential to put your view across in every situation; sometimes just your presence is enough.

It is likely you might need to
change your thinking on this one, to
at least consider the possibility that
the first move you made might in fact
not have been the way to go.

Breathe, stay in the moment, try to let go of that you are seeking to hold and this too shall pass.

Your free-thinking Sagittarian
energy and enthusiasm are infectious
and others adore having you on their
team for just this reason. But it is time
to take a break right now, to allow
things to be as they are. The small
things have a way of working
themselves out, you know.

Actions will speak louder than words, despite the amount of thought you have put into trying to get the words right this time. But tact is not your strong point Sag, as well you know. You are happy to try new things; on this occasion, let that new thing be staying quiet.

Self-congratulation is in order.
Pat yourself on the back Sagittarius;
you are living life well. Let that
warm pleasure and pride in your
achievements rule this moment.

Your natural impatience and desire for change are propelling you forwards too quickly. Resist the urge to pick your path until you are sure you have the right balance between thought and emotion; the wisdom that only comes of head and heart working together will be required in this situation.

This is the perfect place and
time to celebrate the distance
already travelled and how much you
have already managed to achieve,
rather than focusing on what
there still is to do.

Yes, of course you can.
But that doesn't mean that it's the
right decision. Look carefully
before you leap.

It is time to focus on the present Sagittarius. There is no traction to be gained by going over past hurts anymore. Jealousy, resentment and anger will prove baggage too heavy to carry; tending to these needy negatives will hold you back from all you could be achieving.

You are a natural leader and
the trailblazing groundbreaker
of the zodiac, so it can be massively
disorienting when things seem not to
be going your way. But, as ever, there
is a greater plan at work here.
Be patient.

The explanation you give will
be the one that others hear; they have
no way to know what is in your heart
unless you tell them.

Find a way to carry on, even if
this wasn't part of your original plan.
Keep your eye on the prize and
maintain your momentum; slowing
your pace at this point will make
holding your course much more
difficult. Keep moving.

Your charisma and creativity will serve you faithfully. Just be careful not to flit between the options or become distracted and tilt off course – this situation demands a much steadier approach.

It might be that this one seems
to exert an unwelcome hold on you.
If so, stop fighting it; just press pause
and disengage. A little freedom from
the obligation to work it out will make
all the difference and bring some
much-needed clarity.

Energetic and enthusiastic, Sagittarius is ruled by Jupiter, which brings you the best luck and most good fortune of any visible planet. It also reflects the greatest amount of the sun's light, gifting you with a joyful and life-affirming outlook. Now is a good time to remember just how lucky you are.

A powerful fire sign, you tend
to value pace over process. But keep
those feet firmly planted on the
ground, even while you are reaching
for the stars. A steady base will
lengthen your reach.

Of course, anything is possible for such a lightning-quick, razor-sharp Sagittarius. But the direction of approach will make all the difference now, and you will achieve cleaner results if you flip the way you are thinking about this one.

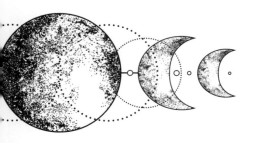

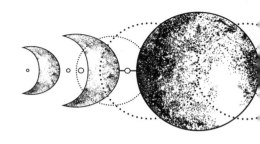

It is extremely tempting to stick to the safe questions, but are you sure this is really the one you want an answer to right now? Think carefully. Ask again.

Try to allow someone else to help this time; they may well surprise you and it might even make things easier.

Keeping your word and holding
a heavy secret safe for someone
will earn you their undying trust
and gratitude.

Your sunny outlook and
commitment to a best-for-all outcome
will ensure you fix your focus on the
task at hand. Your reputation will
benefit, and others will be grateful, too.

Time to try something different. Listen, focus, notice, feel, acknowledge, stay present. While you generally value thinking over feeling, it would be a good idea to take a break from that mind-chatter for a while and simply sink into the moment.

You've no time for those who feed
on petty dramas and won't waste
your energy on the disingenuous or
manipulative. Rightly so. Some things
aren't meant to be. Onwards, no
looking back.

Others sometimes describe your approach as unpredictable (what?!), when in fact you know perfectly well that your dedication to finding the adventure is what makes the fun for everyone else. They should be grateful. Anyway, forget about them; get this done your way.

Your energy, drive and
determination make you a force to be
reckoned with. Have some sympathy
for your opponents, who don't stand a
chance against you, and offer
a compromise.

You dance to your own tune and waste very little time worrying about the opinions of others. But even you need some downtime occasionally, especially if you are to continue pushing ahead with such brilliance. Keep it quiet today, take stock, refuel and you will feel revitalized again in no time.

Time to switch that famous no-nonsense Sagittarius courage on, take a deep breath and pose the right question. Your answer will be right there in front of you, as soon as you are brave enough to ask.

Others may not feel inclined to
bare their souls to you and this might
mean that you don't see the full
picture. Suspend judgement and, if
you really must have your say, consider
all likely outcomes first.

Remember that a true friend is one who tells you what you need to hear, rather than simply what you want to hear. Loyalty and truth go together on this one. Although, granted, it is always a lot more fun to hear things that please you, sugarcoating the facts really isn't your style.

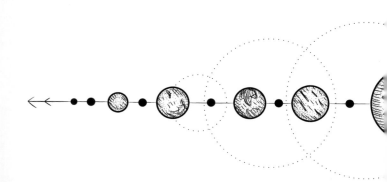

This is a tricky one and there is no 'correct' solution. Others' opinions, were you inclined to consider them, would only complicate matters. Draw on your patience and wait to see what the universe offers up; these things cannot be rushed. You've plenty to get on with in the meantime.

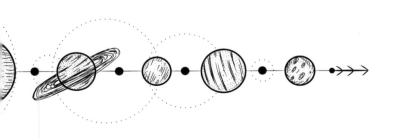

Over-thinking will be your
enemy on this one; resist it, lest it lead
you into never-ending circles of
complication and confusion.

Not every obstacle can be smashed, torn down or burned to the ground – some require a gentler touch. You're an idealist and extremely experience-focused, so use those strengths to engage with this problem. It might not be all bad and expanding your understanding by tracing it back to its roots will be key.

Look for the most elegant solution –
the one that takes the least effort and
creates the fewest ripples.

There is a difference between friendship and flattery. Not all signs agree with you that acknowledging truth is more important than diplomacy. Beware of those simply seeking to smooth their own path.

Your deep understanding of the ways of the world brings a clear-thinking, philosophical approach to everything you do. Resist second-guessing yourself. Your wisdom and strength of purpose will serve you well.

Do not allow your honesty
and impatience to lead you into
hurtful tactlessness – there is
something you urgently need to say,
but it must be spoken in a language
that will be understood.

The situation might not be quite as it seems – engage your natural Sagittarian curiosity and take another look, then pause for thought before you make your decision.

A balance of both head and
heart is required here; resist the urge
to pick a path until you are sure you
have harnessed thought and emotion
in equal measure.

You will have no need of a journey
planner if you simply follow the path
that looks most enticing to you.
Balance your instinct with your
appetite for adventure – it's what
Sagittarius does best.

You're not overly given to introspection Sagittarius – and with so much external excitement to enjoy, who can blame you? But you shouldn't expect that everyone will understand what is truly in your heart unless you tell them. Open up occasionally.

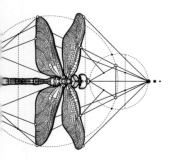

Finding a way around any
obstacles presenting themselves
will be a much cleverer move than
trying to tackle any of them head-on.
Neater, more elegant solutions
are always best!

There are plenty of options here Sagittarius, you just need to figure out which one fits you most comfortably. Take the easier route this time if you can. Enjoying the adventure shouldn't feel like hard work.

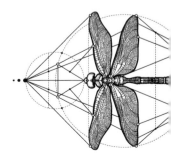

Keep your eyes on the stars
but your feet on the ground, and
take a moment to appreciate just
how amazing the universe is.

It is never too late
for an apology, whether
you are giving
or receiving.

Your constellation tells you all you need to know Sagittarius; you are the centaur archer, half animal instinct and half cool-headed hunter. You are a lucky optimist and freedom-lover, on an eternal quest for truth. Carry on.

Your ability to work quickly and move fast has helped you out of more tight spots than you will probably ever know. Looking back is never high on your agenda Sagittarius, and you have little patience with nostalgia. Honestly, it's working for you – why change?

All this hard work will make sense soon, even if right now it feels like it might not be quite worth it. Something much easier is just around the corner, so you can start enjoying that very soon.

The brightest of the fire signs,
you know better than anyone the
importance of keeping things flowing.
Don't let anything (or anyone) get in
the way of moving forwards.

Truth-seeking travellers have long been afforded a special place in history, culture and tradition. You have an important role to play in shaking up the status quo and challenging preconceptions. Do not shy away from your destiny.

With all the momentum and forward-focus, don't forget that softer, more vulnerable part of yourself: the bit that really matters. It can be hard to stay still and all that introspection can be difficult, even painful sometimes – but it will be worth it.

Perhaps you are spending
too much time and effort trying to
untangle this one, and that's just not
your style. Doubling down on your
efforts will not change the outcome.

This one demands more attention
and time than pure energy and drive.
Don't fail through a simple
lack of focus.

You have the enviable gift of being able to make just about anything fun Sagittarius – allow your creativity and ingenuity to help you again this time.

The perfect opportunity now presents itself – time to sort through your quiver of talents to select the most suitable arrows with which to take aim. You've never been shy, so don't step back from an opportunity that might have been personally crafted just for you.

Slow things down for now – even though it might feel like something must be done immediately, set your impatience aside on this one. You will know when the time is right.

Draw up the strength from the core of yourself. Engage with structure, clarity and intention. Open your heart, dig deep, stay present.

Hold your tongue until you can speak from a place of truth rather than from a desire to force change or have an impact. Only then does what you want to say actually need to be said.

You are ruled by Jupiter,
bringer of miracles and good fortune,
prosperity and courage. Your positive
energy is truly a gift. Acknowledge it,
share it, use it wisely.

Guard against your insecurities, lest they lead you into aggression and vindictiveness. Nothing is more important than maintaining peace with those you love. And resist that impulse to chase those huge wins that carry a correspondingly enormous price for failure. You can have it all, just not this way.

Usually a fiery force and adventure leader, it can be a shock to those around you when frustration takes over. But it is important to allow both sides of your nature the room they need to breathe; neither is good or bad.

They just are.

Know yourself Sagittarius and
keep a mental checklist of the things
you need to do when routine threatens
your usually joyful and adventurous
spirit. Keep moving, seek spontaneity,
talk it through. Above all, be
kind to yourself.

Keeping your heart and mind
open to all possibilities will bring joy to
any quest for new information. When
you feel unstoppable, the world is a
much brighter place.

Like the centaur-archer for whom
Sagittarius is named, you are bold,
curious, adventurous and resourceful.
Use your star-given talents wisely.

Stay open to the possibility of meeting new people and connecting in new ways. There are so many opportunities waiting for you at the moment, keep all paths uncluttered and open the gates so they can find their way to you easily.

The energy of resilience, so intrinsic to your sign, is a dominant force in your engagement with others. Your strength and adaptability are about to really come into their own.

Champion change and resilience
in all you do Sagittarius, transitioning
and clearing to make room for the
new, every step along the way. Always
start with a clean slate.

Your adventurous nature will
twist itself into restlessness and
dissatisfaction if its impulses are
ignored. Nourish this freedom-seeking
part of yourself by allowing plenty of
wide-open spaces and opportunity.
Say 'yes' as often as you can.
Optimism will feed your spirit.

The complicated twists and turns of your own mind will be your ultimate asset, helping you achieve a best-for-everyone outcome here. Let one part handle the thinking and the other plan the action; rise above the detail and it will all be done in no time.

Staying still is simply not in your nature and with big, beautiful Jupiter driving you it's no wonder you prefer a dynamic approach. Just be sure you let others catch up with you once in a while.

A beautiful, forceful, adventurous sign, you're keen to grasp whatever today brings you. Just be careful that all this focus on 'now' doesn't mean that the store-cupboard is completely stripped. Seize the moment, by all means. But remember there is a tomorrow to plan for as well.

Focus on your health, and
happiness will follow.

Teamwork and collaboration are Sagittarian strengths, and when these are combined with your authenticity and enthusiasm there are very few who can resist joining you for the adventure.

It is vital that you are clear and honest (with yourself and others) about your ability to see this one through – don't promise more than you can deliver.

Crossing paths with someone
you usually try to avoid, or perhaps
someone new, might actually make
you stop and think. It will help you
see this situation in a new light.

Seek inspiration in those around you. Once you accept that you cannot control the outcome, and likely have no idea what it might look like yet, you will not have to look too far to find the answer. The universe keeps drumming this lesson home – release your grip and the situation will resolve.

Your usual habit is to move on quickly, and with so much out there still to experience, of course this makes perfect sense. But on this occasion perhaps you might be persuaded to linger a little longer; there are some aspects you haven't yet understood.

Although it is unusual, there are times when you may feel anxious or even afraid and uncertain. There is no fix for this except hunkering down and waiting for it to pass. Accept this time as a gift, seek silence and embrace the opportunity for quiet and introspection.

Secrecy can breed suspicion,
and anyway it's really not your style.
Although keeping things quiet might
feel easier in the short term, your
spirit is more likely to demand a
commitment to openness
and honesty.

Adopt a generous approach to
those you love with regard to time
and advice; you can easily help to ease
their anxiety at the moment. Think of
them rather than yourself.

Open your heart to the possibility of inspiration via a different source. Every interaction offers the opportunity to learn something new.

Allow yourself, and those you love,
some space to process recent events.
Creativity and ingenuity are of vital
importance when it comes to
recalibrating and realigning
your expectations.

You can find adventure and celebration in pretty much any task Sagittarius; this is a particular gift. Share it generously with others, especially those who find the routines of daily life more of a struggle than you do. When tasks weigh heavily on them, your kindness will be more appreciated than you can imagine.

Your charming and engaging Sagittarius personality means you never have a problem making new friends. Putting conscious effort into connecting strongly with people right now will reap some big rewards.

Draw on the creativity of your friends and share your ideas with them in return. Each time one of you succeeds, it's really another win for all of you. Be generous and open as you engage.

Your impulse may well be to stick with your direction of travel until you arrive at that destination you've been striving for. Simple as that. But there is nothing more to be gained with this one; holding on longer than anyone else will simply drag you down.

The fire in your belly drives you forwards and keeps your energy high and forceful. It will be easier to simply allow events to carry you onwards rather than investing too much of your own effort.

Freedom doesn't have to mean detachment Sagittarius; don't confuse the two. And don't be tempted to do something you might regret just because you are feeling that familiar nudge to move on. Take some time to re-evaluate your priorities.

Expand your outlook, set your
course for the horizon and have a
good old-fashioned adventure
Sagittarius. Take a loved one along
for the ride, have some fun.

Open up your prospects and
possibilities by seeking out some new
knowledge Sagittarius; time spent
learning new things is always
an investment.

Stay present in your own positivity Sagittarius. If you feel that people or situations are contriving to pull you into negativity, step around them rather than actively engaging. You might find their relentless dampening too much for your fiery spirit to bear.

Invest some time in the people and places you care about; show them some love and express your appreciation for all the times they have made space for you and held you in place.

Your archer star sign watches over you Sagittarius, and it ensures that you rarely, if ever, miss your mark. The important thing is to first make sure you are actually aiming at the right target.

When you are able to carve out
some time for quiet contemplation, all
will become clear. An added plus will
be the return of that creative spark
you have been so longing to
welcome again.

When heart and head seem
not to be collaborating, there is
a deeper message you need to hear.
Distraction is a sign that your
subconscious is knocking on the door,
requesting some attention.

Independence is a core
Sagittarius trait, a strong flame
that burns at the heart of everything
you do. You find your own path, but
that doesn't mean you should feel
lonely. Quite the opposite.

Your reputation as a trailblazer means that you are frequently sought out by those who respect your free-thinking ways and your clearly defined, individualistic values. Be careful about the wisdom you impart – they may very well decide to act on it.

You need space and flexibility
to do your best work Sagittarius; if
your surroundings are becoming too
claustrophobic it could well be a sign
that it's time for change.

Tackle this problem by agreeing with what is suggested. Allow rather than block. Go along with it and find a way as you move, rather than closing your mind and shutting down a possible solution the first chance you get.

Whether your instinct is telling
you to pull back or charge ahead,
listen and act accordingly.

Do a thorough self-audit and pay particular attention to whether you might perhaps be sacrificing more than you should right now. Is this taking too great a toll on your physical, emotional or mental health... or perhaps all three? If not, fantastic. If so, you will need to prioritize where to best spend your efforts.

Hard work will bring victory,
which has a bit more of a golden ring
to it than merely 'success', doesn't it
Sagittarius? So, keep going.

Routine, organization and sheer
grit will get you over the next hurdle
Sagittarius, but you are going to need
some luck added into the mix as well.
Keep an open mind about what form
that luck might take and welcome
all opportunities.

Ambition and love of success
both play significant roles for you
Sagittarius, but without dedicated
hard work you are going to find
yourself feeling the glow less and less
often. Time to pick up the pace and
stop coasting. A bit of tunnel vision
will do you good right now.

Strongly determined, as well
as a whole heap of fun to be around,
it's easy to understand why you are so
in demand Sagittarius. Be careful to
return the love – if others start feeling
taken for granted, you might face
some problems.

The zodiac's hunter, you follow
an eternal quest for wisdom and truth.
Keep aiming high and you will hit your
mark more often than not.

Now is the time to engage your trademark spontaneity Sagittarius; there is very likely only one best outcome, and you must trust your instincts to guide you straight to it.

Sagittarians are never short of a
few willing helpers – how could
anyone resist the opportunity to join in
the fun? Ultimately, whether they offer,
or you ask, it doesn't really matter as
long as you reach your goal.

Resist second-guessing
yourself Sagittarius, trust your
intuition. It rarely lets you down.

Your intense curiosity fuels you
Sagittarius, and your hunger for new
experiences, information, friends,
travel and knowledge seems insatiable.
Remember to collect and treasure as
you go rather than thoughtlessly
discarding, to save you unwittingly
letting go of something precious
without realizing it.

Your strength and determination are powerful forces Sagittarius; you have all you need to succeed already within you. Focus on the task at hand, allowing yourself to become fully absorbed in it, and soon enough your confidence will grow and your doubts will melt away – you won't even remember what you had been worried about.

Be careful Sagittarius, and
examine your reasons closely before
making a move or building those
flames up too high.

All that energy you have invested will pay off as positives and rewards start to find their way to your door. Be sure you allow yourself the time and headspace to truly relish them – you deserve it.

Bags packed again so soon Sagittarius? Sometimes others have difficulty understanding your need to be constantly on the move, but the thrill of adventure is what keeps you going. The plain truth is, it's just your journey.

Now is a good time to release
that tension Sagittarius, and to lay
down some of that weight you have
been carrying around. Do not hold
onto anything that is not serving
you – a much lighter, breezier flow
is required if you are going to
keep that spark alight.

As a fire sign Sagittarius,
burning bright is just the way you
glow. If others feel inferior, growing
their own self-esteem should be their
first priority rather than trying
to dull your shine.

It's all about energy with you at the moment Sagittarius... although, really, when is it not? A fire sign, and ruled by Jupiter too, there so often seems to be a load of significant things going on for you. Try to keep on top of all the energy, rather than letting it zip about erratically. Harness and direct it.

Be sure that all those amazing people who are always helping you out know how much you appreciate them. Acknowledge and be grateful for those who gave you a hand up.

Your value system might differ
slightly from someone else's, but they
don't have to live your life.
Run your own race.

Fixing on definites and making firm plans might not be in the stars for you right now Sagittarius... if it feels too difficult, let it go. There will be time to try again later.

You are an independent and philosophical soul Sagittarius, but too much distance can start to cool that flame... never good for a fire sign.

If you are feeling suspicious,
or perhaps even paranoid, it might
be that you have been positioning
yourself too far from the centre of the
action – always a danger for such an
independent sign. Realign yourself
with what's going on and reassert your
presence to remind others
that you're there.

Resist the temptation to add
a bit more fire to this one; just
watch and wait.

If you are facing problems with others at the moment, be sure that your response deals cleanly with behaviours, circumstances and events rather than diving down into an attack on anyone's basic human essence. Issues outside your frame of reference may very well have played a part. Tread carefully.

Using flattery to get what you
want is an almost ubiquitous human
technique... but employ it sparingly.
Pull the same tactic too many times
on the same target and they may start
to suspect your motives.

The art of conversation is a particular Sagittarian skill, but at the moment it's a good idea to stick to face-to-face communication as much as possible. Where there is a chance that what you say might be misinterpreted, your body language will save the day.

Keep your eyes open, take an interest and notice everything. Store whatever you find away for the time being and wait for the next phase. More information will follow and it will better contextualize what you are learning now.

Stay awake to what is going on around you Sagittarius; you are more observant than most people anyway and with that extra vigilance, you will certainly catch some important signs that others might miss. Watch, note and wait. Your observations will bring you extra leverage or advantage that might prove very useful soon.

There is no immediate urgency to
act on what you know, despite outside
pressure or a sense of time passing.
Others may be more interested in how
events will benefit their own strategy,
and what is true today should still be
true tomorrow. Patience.

Want and need are very
different Sagittarius, and when forces
of desire are compelling you to act
you should take extra care to be sure
of your motivation. Material items may
not actually be particularly useful; in
fact, they may prove to be just the
opposite. But investing for the
future in some way... now that
could be worth it.

Keep resources accessible and available Sagittarius – this could mean money, the help of friends or support of family, an aspect of your health or wellbeing plan, or some particular equipment or technology you rely on. You may not need them right away, but if you do you will be pleased to have everything in place.

Stress and strain might be stirring
up some difficult emotions Sagittarius,
either for you or someone you care
about... or possibly both. Either way,
do everything you can to keep the
mood light and the vibe fun. Now
is not the time for deep
and meaningful.

A straightforward and honest approach will be more beneficial than a calculated conversation designed to manipulate. The person you are engaging with will be relieved and pleased to see a more grown-up you, one they can engage with more efficiently and matter-of-factly. This will be to everyone's benefit.

Your super-energy needs a physical outlet Sagittarius, otherwise you find yourself spinning in circles with your body and emotions feeling frazzled and sparking off in all directions. Do yourself (and everyone else) a favour and head out for a run or a long walk to straighten yourself out again.

Sometimes the best things come
out of the worst things. It doesn't need
to make sense. Set attempts to control
or influence aside for now Sagittarius,
and hold onto hope.

Being out of sync might cause
you to feel disconnected and less
trusting of those you know. Reset your
usually optimistic approach with a
shake-up: plan your next trip or
another kind of adventure
closer to home.

Sagittarians are excellent storytellers, bringing the perfect combination of wit and wisdom to entertain your audience. Don't get so caught up in the performance that you forget your task and purpose.

Authenticity is your best approach right now and, given that you are such a truth-teller anyway, it's the only way for you to feel you are acting with integrity. Making it up will put you on the back foot in more ways than one.

If you have a point to make, be straightforward and finesse the facts as little as possible Sagittarius. Deliver the information. It is up to them to decide how to take it.

Being the archer of the zodiac is about to come in pretty handy. Shut out distractions and concentrate your aim – you will need complete focus to strike your target this time.

Doors tend to open for you Sagittarius; if you have to give them a little push now and then, or oil the hinges a bit, so be it.

Keep an open mind and a receptive heart right now. Make a plan, by all means, but accept that it may need to change several times along the way before you get to where you want to be.

Build some self-care into your daily routine Sagittarius. Knowing that your schedule means burnout is not impossible, give some careful consideration to taking care of yourself with exercise, meditation or some good old-fashioned downtime.

Staying grounded and balanced
is essential if you are to keep up this
pace Sagittarius; don't fool yourself
that you can do everything and burn
the candle at both ends without
paying a price.

Don't allow yourself to be pressured or manipulated into making the wrong decision. As a fire sign, it's not unknown for you to burn hot on the impulsivity front. Don't let anyone take advantage of that inclination for their own ends.

Patience and thorough research
will be rewarded Sagittarius. Throwing
caution to the winds, not so much.
Invest carefully. Good things come
to those who wait.

If your instincts tell you that you are being short-changed, you have every right to insist on answers Sagittarius. Don't let up until you are sure you are being told the truth.

First published in Great Britain in 2021 by
Greenfinch
An imprint of Quercus Editions Ltd
Carmelite House
50 Victoria Embankment
London EC4Y 0DZ

An Hachette UK company

A CIP catalogue record for this book is available
from the British Library

HB ISBN 978-1-52941-236-9

Every effort has been made to contact copyright holders.
However, the publishers will be glad to rectify in future editions any
inadvertent omissions brought to their attention.

Quercus Editions Ltd hereby exclude all liability to the extent
permitted by law for any errors or omissions in this book and for any loss,
damage or expense (whether direct or indirect) suffered by a third party
relying on any information contained in this book.

10 9 8 7 6 5 4 3 2 1

Designed by Ginny Zeal
Cover design by Andrew Smith
Text by Susan Kelly
All images from Shutterstock.com

Printed and bound in China.

FSC
www.fsc.org

MIX
Paper from
responsible sources
FSC® C016973

Papers used by Greenfinch are from well-managed forests
and other responsible sources.